SENIOR GRADUATION

"What Every Senior Needs to Know About Life After Graduation"

Author: Sheriff Dan Johnson
Copyright 2017
All Rights Reserved

Published by the Ridge Enterprise Group
(AR/USA)
ISBN: 978-0-9962390-3-5

Contents

Dedication

I dedicate this book to my family, my son William Daniel Johnson, III (Trey); my daughter Lezlie, and my grandson Christopher. And to my parents, Dan and Earline, who laid the foundation for all the good things in my life.

Acknowledgement

I would like to thank my friend Mark Moore for his help in editing this book. He is a writer too. You may want to check out some of his books. For example if you are struggling with some things in Genesis then see "Early Genesis, the Revealed Cosmology". If you are struggling with forming a philosophy about government and politics then his two books on political philosophy, "Localism" and "Localism Defended" might help you.

My Start and Yours

The year 1981 must seem like ancient history to you. It was the year I stood in your shoes as a newly-minted High School graduate. Even though it was so long ago I remember that day like it was yesterday. The world is a lot different now, but some things don't change. The emotions that you feel today are probably very much like those that I felt all those long years ago.

Well, maybe a little different. The economy you enter today is harder than the one I entered. When I was standing in your shoes I was full of confidence about the future. I could not wait to get out there and "tear it up." And eventually I did, thanks in part to some wise counsel. It came in the unlikely form of Mr. Ulis Huffine.

During Christmas vacation (the schools still called it that back then) my dad and I went to the Farmer's Co-Op. This was in my hometown of Marianna, Arkansas. We were shopping for some supplies when I saw the elderly Mr. Huffine just sitting in the co-op. Now in small towns like Marianna everyone knows everyone else's business. And so it was that even as an eighteen year-old I understood that this older gentleman in coveralls sitting by the sacks of cattle-feed was a rich man. He was probably the richest man in town. Even though it was hard to keep secrets in that town, no one at the time knew how just much money

1

Mr. Huffine had. We just knew that it was a lot. I asked him a question that day and I think his answer changed my financial future. I will talk more about that in the next chapter.

As someone who is a recent graduate or about to graduate, you are probably thinking "what will I do for a living"? The early choices you make can help you succeed in life or can forever be a burden which will destroy your financial independence. Sometimes I think it is a shame that the decisions people make when they are so young still affect their lives decades later, but that is the way the world is made. So it's important to get good advice wherever you can find it.

Even though I have said all that, there are many different kinds of people and many different ways to have a secure financial future. You may choose a field and find that you don't like it. You may choose a field but another door opens that you like better. You may grow as a person so that the kind of job which was right for you at one age is unsuitable when you get older.

Many people find themselves feeling the need to "re-boot" and start over professionally. What is most critical is arranging your finances so that you *can* start over if you feel the need to or see what will eventually be a better opportunity. It's all about keeping your options open. That way you can be the one to take advantage of opportunity when it passes by.

When I was a boy I dreamt of being a Sheriff, a dream fueled in part by the movie "Walking Tall". It was loosely based on the true story of a rural Sheriff who took on corruption in his county. But I also realized that I needed more than dreams, I needed a steady income. So I took up the first of four professional careers that I have had in my lifetime- I started off modestly because it was my best opportunity which was available without going into debt. I became an Emergency Medical Technician.

I know a lot of young people want to hop straight into following their dream, and a few can pull it off. Most of us will be in a better position to achieve our dream if we start somewhere more practical, and then move toward our dreams from a secure financial foundation.

If you handle it right then it doesn't mean that you give up on your dream. It just means that you don't have to compromise your core values to obtain your dream because you have something to fall back on. Starting with a more conventional trade can also add richness and experience that you can take with you when it is time to follow your dream.

I was an EMT for seventeen years but I also kept my hand in law enforcement. We dealt with situations in tandem with the police on many occasions. Heck, I even delivered a baby at home once, and I think the grandmother still believes that I am a doctor! Eventually I ran for constable, which is not much of an office these days but it was a start.

I also worked for years as a trainer/instructor for Eastman/Kodak. Their main product at the time was film, something which was once in widespread use but hardly

3

exists anymore. And then one day the Sheriff's job opened up unexpectedly, due to scandal. There was no favorite to replace the incumbent. It was a perfect chance for an outsider, even though my resume for that office was pretty thin.

Fortunately despite our modest income I had structured our family finances so that when opportunity knocked, I was able to open the door and go to it. I campaigned relentlessly, starting with the most remote parts of the county and working my way up to the county seat. The courthouse gang did not give me much of a chance in that crowded field of seven, and that was the way I wanted it until it was too late to throw mud at me! The rural folks appreciated my coming to their door while the other six candidates were all sucking up to the same prominent citizens in one city.

I found that the more trouble I went to in order to ask for someone's vote, the more likely I was to get it. One time I heard voices under a house that was being built so I crawled under there too. I found two guys installing ductwork and asked them for their votes. They said that anyone who went to that much trouble was sure to be a good worker and that they were going to vote for me! Just because I did not go for my dream right away didn't mean that I was not willing to go after it hard when the time was right. That's the key though, you have to be ready, and the circumstances have to be favorable. I surprised the court house bunch and won the election.

Starting in January of 2001 I served as the Sheriff of Independence County, Arkansas. I ran on a platform of shutting down the meth distribution and production networks and I kept my campaign promises. They tried bribery, and they tried to set me up in a compromising position with a woman, and they tried to entice me into gambling and other illegal activities. When none of that worked, someone made a credible and specific death threat on my two children, Trey and Lezlie. I was already learning that my dream was not all that I imagined it to be. Some of the most "respectable" folks in the county seemed unhappy at the way I was closing down the meth houses. The death threat was the last straw. I announced that I would not run for re-election.

I think young people who are drawn to politics, or the ministry for that matter, without first establishing another career to fall back on are setting themselves up to be placed in a terrible position. If you think you can't walk away then you are going to be tempted to do whatever it takes to stay in, even if in some corner of your heart you know that it isn't right. You will put yourself in a much better position to do long term good in those kinds of callings if you know in your heart and head that you can do something else for a while if need be.

The other lesson there is that sometimes you have to know when the dream you wanted is not really what you thought it was. You have to know who you really are and when to let go. I was, first and foremost, the father of my children. Besides all that, I figured if I could not do the job I wanted to do then at least I could seek another long-term goal that I had. That was to make the amount of money that I wanted to make. When I was young I had set as my financial goal to earn an annual income of $250,000. That financial goal was in conflict with my career goal of being a County Sheriff – at least an honest one!

Once I left public office, I went after that financial goal, and, give or take a few grand, achieved it before the age of fifty. Even more importantly, I have managed to live in such a way as to get accumulated capital to "work for me." There are people who make that same amount of money who still don't have great wealth. If they lost their income for a year it would ruin them. Don't be one of those "high-earners". They must feel like hamsters on a tread-mill! I want to help you be the kind who can use their wealth to leverage themselves into the kind of situations that they want. The key is to arrange things so that you are always in position to walk away if a deal is not right for you.

Mr. Huffine: A Fifteen Minute "Doctorate" in Finance

It was during the two week vacation in December of 1980 and my dad, Dan Johnson Sr., and I walked into the local Farmers Co-Op. I had no idea that I was about to get a lesson in finance that would forever change my life. As dad and I walked in the door Mr. Huffine sat there all alone, chewing tobacco in his faded holey torn coveralls.

I understand that young people sometimes do not want to bother with the elderly, even those who have already achieved everything that the young person hopes to achieve in life. Today we get a lot of advice off of the internet from people trying to sell us something. Either that or we talk to friends who are about our age, and have been through similar experiences and institutions. In other words, they haven't had the chance to see it much different than we have!

I think that is too limiting. To really get better, we have to broaden our view and talk to people who have already done what we hope to do, even if they are outside of what we would normally think of as our 'peer group'. Not only will reaching out allow you to gain valuable insight from people who know more than you do, they are better to network with than someone who is "just like you" on a lot of levels. Networking with people like you doesn't add as much to your connections and opportunities as networking with people who are ahead of you!

I am not saying to "suck up." That is phony and the smart older people can spot that a mile away. I am saying that extending genuine goodwill toward people beyond those you would normally associate with is the right thing to do for you and them. Learning how to navigate among different sorts of people has been one of the keys to my success. I have negotiated a business deal with a farmer one day and a city lawyer the next. Moving among different ages and types of people is a developed skill and I urge you to start developing it.

Here I was, about to graduate from High School and start to become an adult. There was a man in front of me that was the richest guy in town. Not that we had cell phones back in that day, but I wasn't going to just fiddle with my cell phone. I wanted to take this opportunity to visit with a man who had "been there, done that". So I turned to my father and said "Dad I will sit here and visit with Mr. Huffine while you get our supplies".

Mr. Huffine asked me how I had been doing and if I was ready for a big Christmas. I responded with a positive outlook, and mentioned to him that I was excited about graduating. Then I asked him the key question.

I said, "Mr. Huffine, I am about to graduate in five months and if you were to give me one piece of advice to be financially successful like you some day, what would that piece of advice be"? He sat there very quiet for a brief moment and said, "You know that is a great question, Dan. I have learned a great deal about money over my life but I guess if I only had time to share with you the most important part about financial success in my life it would be this: If you can't pay cash for what you buy, *don't buy it*. Don't buy it under *any* circumstances."

I understand that Mr. Huffine died in the early 1990's. After buying everything he ever really wanted in life he passed on and left many millions of dollars to his family. He was a true millionaire next door. I use that phrase deliberately. There is a book titled "The Millionaire Next Door." It was published in 1997 by two PhDs., Dr. Danko and Dr. Stanley. They studied the millionaires of America for twenty years.

After two decades of study they learned that the rich appear to be poor and the poor appear to be rich. Many people with a net worth of over a million dollars own their own modest home in middle class neighborhoods. On the other hand, most of the inhabitants of upscale neighborhoods with huge homes are up to their eyeballs in debt and don't really own those homes or even have any equity in them to speak of. Basically, out of 100 so called rich people in an elite neighborhood, only *four* can truly afford to be there. The other 96% or ninety-six families only *appear* to be wealthy enough to be in that neighborhood. They are living above their true means and failing to build any wealth while doing so. Do you get the picture?

While I greatly appreciate the work of those two professors and recommend that book, the principle they "discovered" was actually already in writing over twenty centuries ago in the pages of the Proverbs of King Solomon. That's right. You can find it written in your Holy Bible. Proverbs 13:7 (NIV) reads:

"One person pretends to be rich, yet has nothing;
another pretends to be poor, yet has great wealth."

People have been "putting on airs" for a long time. People have been trying to pass themselves off as rich and important when they are not for a long time. Wise people have been modest and reluctant to display their wealth for a long time. Instead, of consuming their wealth in loud displays which only show how much debt they can get into, the wise forgo such things and save their earnings. This allows them to guard against the disaster of losing everything in a day of misfortune and then allows them to build true wealth slowly over time.

Young ladies, imagine two guys are courting you and one has a fancy new car with a big car payment and the other has an old junker that is paid for and a savings account. I advise you to tell the former "goodbye" and seriously give the latter a chance! That fellow is a serious candidate to give someone a good life.

I realize that this sort of talk is contrary to "conventional wisdom". Frankly I think most of what passes for "conventional wisdom" these days is for suckers. This notion that you need a high credit score and that a credit score is what makes the world go around is nonsense. Getting a high credit score comes from getting heavily in debt and then paying that debt. Just like the principle about poor people trying to be rich and vice-versa was written in the scriptures long ago, so was the bottom line about debt. Proverbs 22:7 (NIV) reads:

"The rich rule over the poor,
  and the borrower is slave to the lender."

That is just the truth in plain words. Maybe so plain that we don't want to face up to the truth of them. Maybe it's not how things ought to be, but it is how things are and have been since civilization began. Sure outright slavery is illegal, but if you spend all day working to pay for things that you still don't really own for the benefit of the one you borrowed from in order to buy it, then I have to ask- how "free" are you? Living on credit means that you are a slave to those to whom you owe that life. Having a high credit score just means that you have been a good slave! A "credit rating" is actually a "slave rating" so that those who would bid on you, on your future earnings, have a better idea about what they ought to pay for you! Don't get me wrong, you should pay your bills. What I am cautioning you against is any rationale or con that would convince you that going into debt is a "good thing" or a healthy thing.

I want to give you an example of what I am talking about. I have a close friend in his 30's that has about a hundred rental properties in Little Rock, Arkansas. He lives by a rule to not have any personal debt, but he is all for business debt. Now when you hear that this young man owns about one hundred rental properties you think "wow that is a wealthy young man." But that represents the "asset" side of his business ledger. He also has a "liability" side.

Dan Johnson

By age thirty-five he owed about $2.7 million dollars in real estate debt. This translates to about $28,000 in monthly payments. His business plan model calls for a fifteen year pay off. This amount of property has the potential to generate about $40,000 a month. That is if they are nearly all rented, and the renters are paying. The $12,000 a month difference allows him to hire a full time manager and a few part time employees. Even if he is only gets to keep a little of that income now, once he pays off the jumbo loan in fifteen years he will get to keep the $28,000 in rent each month that he now uses to pay those mortgages!

If he gets there without leveraging again, he will be a wealthy man by the time he is out of his forties. If all goes well. If anything goes wrong in the next fifteen years he could easily be ruined. Keep in mind while the banker is smiling and treating you like a best friend at his office and slapping you on the back with his right hand, that all changes if you miss one payment. It is only then you discover that he has a knife in his left hand.

My friend and I went to breakfast one morning and he looked like he had seen a ghost. I said, "Are you sick?" He looked green. He looked like he was about to run into the bathroom. Finally, he shared enough that I understood that he was about three days away from his mortgage being due on the jumbo loan and he was about $12,000 shy on his monthly payment. Maybe the renters were not paying, maybe he had other expenses. I don't know. I just know that if he missed that payment he would go from the "owner" of one hundred rental properties to a man who had nothing. The point is wealth comes slowly. Fast cash built on "leverage" can destroy you and bury you into a debt hole that you can't get out of ever.

Some way and somehow, the $12,000 came in just in time and he was off the hook *that* month. My same friend paid off his mansion note loan because he does not like personal debt. But he added the refinance to the 100 rental homes he had. And the bank included under the terms of that loan his personal liability beyond the collateral of the rent houses. This means if he defaults on the rentals then even his personal home will be sold by the bank.

Bottom line, my buddy will be wealthy with all of his "leveraging" someday *if* all goes well with the economy and he can maintain the juggle of the empty houses with no money coming in the coffers. However, he also has the potential to lose it all. He could easily wind up fifty years old with nothing. And every month in between now and then he will have to sweat whether or not that next payment comes in. That can't be good for one's long-term health, and what is good health worth?

It really comes down to how much of a gambler you are. I favor peace of mind over the thrill of dodging bullets month after month. Peace of mind is a tremendous benefit in life. My friend is a natural gambler. He has gone on to get in deeper. He has 250 rentals now and $4.6 million in debt. I believe he told me that he will pay about $50,000 a month in payments. The day he pays that loan off, if it comes, he will be a wealthy man. I hope it comes, but understand this: It won't be because he was wiser than anyone else, or smarter than anyone else. It will be because he rolled the dice and won.

13

For everyone who leverages and wins there will be another, probably many others, who lose and lose big. Just like with a casino, the house always wins and the house is the bank. Those who walk out of a casino with a big pile of money were those who were luckiest, not those who were wisest. Most people who take their advice on how to build wealth will fail. Most who take my advice will succeed. It may take longer, but it will also stay longer.

Wealth gained by leverage is never really safe, because when you get it that way it is hard to know when to "walk away from the table". The temptation of someone who gambles and wins is always to gamble again- until eventually they wind up losing. What if my young friend wins his bet and winds up owning $4.6 million worth of rental property by age forty-seven? Will he quit there, or will he be tempted to leverage again and go for $10 million? If he keeps doing that, eventually he is going to lose because in that game only the house (the bank) always wins.

One of the richest men in America at the time of the stock market crash of 1929 was Jesse Livermore. He had already made a fortune shorting stocks in the 1907 crash, and he called the crash of 1929 as well. He was worth $100 million in 1929 dollars, an immense sum. But he was a gambler. He couldn't quit while he was ahead. His whole life trained him to keep leveraging, to keep betting. Ten years later he was down to perhaps five million dollars and he took his life by his own hand, feeling like a failure. Such is the fruit of wealth gained by speculation and leverage. Not even the genius Sir Isaac Newton could succeed in the long term by speculating in stocks. When he lost much of his fortune doing so he quipped that he could calculate the course of the stars, but not the madness of men!

The Truth about Credit – Even for a Home

The two most commonly-purchased big-ticket items in America are cars and homes. Both of these purchases are the American dream and the bigger the better. Banks will generally allow you to take a home loan which is three times your house-hold income. For example if you make $50,000 annually the bank will offer up to a one hundred and fifty thousand dollar loan home.

Normally they also insist that you come up with a twenty percent down payment, though plenty of programs are available which waive that requirement. After all, most banks these days don't keep the income stream for the loan. They bundle up the rights to the payments on mort-gages and sell them as "securities". So ultimately they don't even care much if you can really pay it. They will loan you money that you can't pay back, sell the right to collect the payments to some other sucker, and then go find someone else to lure into borrowing too much so they can do it again.

There are ways to get into a home with little money or no money down, especially for "first time home buyers". That does not always mean that it's a good idea!

Waiving the requirement for a 20% down payment comes with a catch. You have to pay for extra insurance, but not insurance which pays you. It pays the bank if they have to foreclose on you and don't get all of their money back when they re-sell the house! Once you get twenty percent equity in the home you no longer have to carry that insurance because by then they figure if they have to foreclose on you they can get the money back since you have already paid back 20% of the original principal. You may be shocked though to find out how long it takes, and how much you have to pay in interest, before you have even paid back 20% of the principal amount.

If you saw a bank advertising a home loan for 60% interest would you take it? How about 70% or even 90%? And yet depending on how you calculate interest, many mortgages wind up taking that much of your payments just in interest for years on end. A young couple may think that they are "buying a house" when they make their monthly house payment, but in truth most of what they are doing is paying the bank interest, not building equity.

Even though the loan may say "Six percent APR" that does not mean that six percent of your payments go to interest and the rest to paying on principal /equity. The interest payments on those loans are "front loaded." That is, you are paying the interest first. Let me give you a specific example.

Let's say you took a thirty year mortgage for $115,000 at six percent interest. According to a standard amortization chart at the end of the first year you would have made twelve mortgage payments totaling $8,273.80. Since the loan was at six percent interest you might think that six percent of that went to interest and 94% went to principal. But that is only true of the 1/30th part of the loan that applies to this year! They charged you pure interest on the other twenty-nine slices of that loan, each representing a year of principal payments you have not made yet.

So only $1,412.21 went toward principal and $6,861.58 was paid in interest. After paying $8,273.80 you still owe $113,587.79 in principal on the loan. The equity you built up that first year is just a blip compared to the total amount of the loan. If the heater breaks and you have to borrow to fix it you could actually be in the hole. That is, you could owe more on the house than you did when you started after a year of making payments!

Ten years must seem like a long time to someone your age, and it is a long time. It can seem especially long when you are making payments that are mostly interest for all of those years. Under this completely typical scenario, at the end of ten years of making payments you have paid the bank $82,730. You would still owe the bank $96,238.58 plus interest! That's right, less than twenty percent of the loan principal has been paid down after ten years. Only $2,200 or so of your payments during that tenth year went to principal, almost $6,000 was paid in interest!

When do your mortgage payments go more to principal than to interest? The balance tips, barely, during the nineteenth year of the note. If you are about to graduate high school that means you are either under nineteen or barely nineteen. So it will take as long as you have been alive just to get that note to the point where more of your payment each month is going to actually building equity in your home rather than just paying the bank their interest.

If you and your spouse manage to go thirty years without a big lean period (when you can't pay the mortgage due to unemployment or illness) you might get that house loan paid off. But even in that rosy scenario you will have paid about $250,000 for that $115,000 loan. Actually you could have paid more than that because there are other fees involved in taking out a loan. If you did not make a hefty down payment then you also would have had to buy mortgage insurance until your equity was sufficient. In the meantime you may have to pass up on seeking better financial opportunities in other places because you have this home tying you down. Check that, homes don't tie someone down. A paid-for home is not the problem. Mortgages are the problem!

Now I understand that most people, especially young people, cannot purchase a home with cash up-front. And there are a lot of folks that know they are in a stable situation and know at least the area where they want to put down roots. If this is you, then the second best thing to not having any debt is having much less debt than you could have. That is, have a manageable amount of debt so that there is so much "slack in the line" that even if life gives you a few setbacks you can still swing it.

This means that when the bank tells you that you can qualify for a loan of $150,000 you only borrow half that and no more, even if it means taking far less house than you "want". What you really want is something that you can pay for without being a source of stress to you over the next thirty years! You want a home that you can keep as long as you want it instead of losing it when you hit a rough patch. So when they offer you a $150,000 loan, you say "no" and only borrow $75,000.

Even when the bank is evaluating how much they are willing to loan you, I urge you to ask them to evaluate your loan qualification amount based on one income and not two. Even if you are not thinking about children right now, life has a way of throwing surprises at you. One of you may get ill, injured, or laid off sometime over the next three decades and the other spouse may need to serve as the sole breadwinner for a time. The natural desire to have children usually will kick in as you get older.

Don't be one of those people forced to put your children in day-care at a very young age because you were counting on two paychecks to keep your head above water. The decision on whether or not to do that is very personal and you are never really sure which way you want to go on it until you get there. That is why you want to arrange your life so that it is a *choice* and not a necessity! Too many people are seeking luxury homes and not considering the non-monetary luxury life-style of freeing the wife to be a full-time homemaker, especially when you have young children. Taking a lesser house than you can get gives you the luxury of not being under so much debt- which opens up a lot of other options for you. If you must get a home loan, find out how much the bank will loan you on your best income (not both incomes) and only borrow half *that* amount or less!

I have a friend who followed this path in purchasing a home many years ago. He is a smart and capable man, but he has not been as blessed as I have been as far as consistently earning large amounts of money. He has had his ups-and-downs career-wise. But because he followed this plan, he was able to not only buy a home, but he paid off his thirty-year loan in only fifteen years. If he had taken out as big a loan as the bank had let him, he surely would have lost the house during the down times.

In the good times he made extra payments which he directed specifically toward paying down the principal. Honestly it was the best investment he could have made because it had a guaranteed return. He did not have to pay the interest on that money for the remainder of the thirty years. Unless your employer matches on a 401K, there is really no reason to have a 401K or dabble in stocks until your mortgage is paid off. Make sure any loan you enter into allows you to pay off the principal early without penalty!

In the lean times my friend just made his payment, which was very low because it was a one-bathroom house under 1200 square feet. That low payment helped him make it through those times without falling behind on his loan. Now he has no mortgage payment at all and is in great shape to survive the next layoff or whatever comes along. He and his wife, a full-time home-maker, have three children. It's a tight fit, but he is living proof that we don't need as much home as we, or a real estate agent, think that we need.

My last point about buying a home is to make living around good people a priority. When you purchase a home in a community you are casting your lot with those people. Is the city government corrupt? Are the neighbors a mess? Living around decent folks is an underappreciated perk that government will have a hard time putting a taxable value on.

If you think I am tight-fisted when it comes to spending money on a house, well I am way worse when it comes to buying a car! I will say again what I have said before. Young ladies, imagine two guys are courting you and one has a fancy new car with a big car payment and the other has an old junker that is paid for and a savings account. I advise you to tell the former "goodbye" and seriously give the latter a chance! That fellow is a serious candidate to give someone a good life. Vehicles depreciate, that is lose their value, very quickly. Thirty years down the road your house will likely be worth more than you paid for it, but in only three years a car is not worth half of what you paid for it.

One of the things the Doctors who wrote "The Millionaire Next Door" noticed was that these millionaires overwhelmingly purchased used cars rather than new ones. The "smart money" only puts a minimal amount of capital into depreciating assets like vehicles. Especially while they are building wealth, they just get good basic transportation and leave the fancy new cars to people who are poor but pretending to be rich, like it talks about in Proverbs.

23

I suggest that until you can pay cash for a car you should follow my 57 Chevy 36 plan. Never look at a vehicle any newer than 5 years old. Don't purchase a vehicle that costs more than $7,000 and if you must finance never finance past 36 months. Twelve months would be better. Cars depreciate so fast that you are "underwater" on longer loans. That is, the car becomes worth less than the money that you paid for it. This means if you get in a pinch you can't sell the car and pay off then entire loan. You could find yourself with car payments and no car!

And that brings me to the last point that I wanted to make about cars, and this one is for young couples. You don't necessarily each need a car. Maybe you could forgo two cars and get one that was a little more upscale (but not new!). That way you are only paying for once insurance policy, one set of taxes and tags, and only one depreciating asset! It is likely that each of you brought a car into the relationship, but one of them will be wearing out soon. Consider trying to make it work with one car if you can. It is possible to get by with one car, especially if you decide that the wife will concentrate on homemaking while the children are young.

More than One Way to Get Educated

I suspect that most of the readers of this little book are high school students or recent graduates. Over three million American students graduate from High School each year. Now comes the part where you have to figure out what you are going to do for a living and how you are going to make it happen.

When it comes to a career and success there are several general factors which must be considered: Aptitude, Preparation, and Passion. Aptitude just means how naturally good you are at something. Preparation is the honing of whatever natural abilities you might have and includes education and training, as well as seeking out the right opportunities and separating yourself from the poor ones. Passion is what you enjoy doing. Ideally, all three factors should come together and build on one another for your successful career.

Sometimes there are people who have aptitude at something they hate. They are good at it, they just don't like it. You may find yourself in this position at some point because you have to pay the bills. Work does not have to be fun, that's why they call it "work" and have another word for "play". Stick with it when you have to, but if you can find a way to develop a passion for something marketable you will be a lot happier than doing something you hate every day just for the money. People who get good enough at their hobbies to turn it into a profession are among the most fortunate people on earth. They get paid to do something that they love.

Sometimes that doesn't work out. There is a fellow I know of who I will call Roger. He is a good artist and he loves art. But he's not a great artist, and to make a living at art you usually need to be a great artist or in the case of some of these low-talent bums I see these days you need to be great at self-promotion. Nor did he receive much education or training other than some apprenticeship. He was mostly self-taught. He had the passion, but not quite the aptitude, and he did not first get the preparation which would have maximized the aptitude that he did have.

Ultimately I think he would have been more satisfied with a conventional career and doing his art as a side-line. He did not have a good balance of the three factors that should be considered: Aptitude, Passion, and Preparation. As a result he spent his working life frustrated, even though it was doing something that he loved. Honest self-assessment is too rare these days despite its value. If you get in the habit of telling yourself the truth about yourself instead of making excuses or blaming others, it will serve you much better in life than kidding yourself.

You may never reach the point where your hobby becomes your profession. But whatever honest job you do, make up your mind to do it with as much excellence and passion as you can muster, whether your boss is likeable or unlikeable. The great American industrialist Henry Ford had a lot of great quotes in his life. He said things like "If I had asked people what they wanted, they would have said 'faster horses.'" There is another quote which is widely attributed to him even if he never actually said it. That is "The biggest mistake that any man can make is to think that they are working for someone else."

Ultimately, it's true, unless we are Christians. In that case Ephesians chapter six tells us to do our work "as unto the Lord". Even in a secular job, we are ultimately working for Him because our work is a part of our witness and character development. In our profession we are to try our best to do whatever we are doing right and with a good attitude. That same chapter tells us to do it whether those who are over us are reasonable or unreasonable! That does not make a lot of sense on the surface, and it is against the spirit of our age, but I have noticed that people who apply the principles laid out in Ephesians Chapter six over time develop habits and attitudes which produce for them options that they would not otherwise have. In time, they may convert an unreasonable boss to a reasonable one, or more likely, they will have choices and be able to go to work for someone who is better to serve.

So that is a few choice words about passion and aptitude. The third factor is preparation and by nature it is one which needs more detail and commentary. I want to preface it by saying that being able to communicate is essential to success in almost any career. If you can't speak well, or write well, it is going to be a tough row to hoe for you in the professional world. There are a lot of high schools

27

today who turn out graduates who have shortcomings in these areas. Fortunately your skill in these things is not "set in stone" on the day you graduate high school. You can get better at them for years to come. Communicating can be improved by skill, development, and practice. Don't just decide that you can't read or write or speak well because of what you experienced in High School.

The greatest orator in ancient Greece was said to be a man named Demosthenes who lived centuries before Christ walked the earth. Even though he achieved fame as a speaker, as a young man he had some kind of speech impediment. Rather than deciding that he just wasn't a good speaker, Demosthenes developed several exercises to improve his public speaking skills. He gave practice speeches with pebbles in his mouth to force him to really concentrate on pronunciation. He practiced speaking over the roar of the ocean's waves to teach himself how to project.

His life came to a tragic end. He did not succeed in his political goals, but he did succeed in overcoming his handicaps and his story is inspirational for people even all of these centuries later.

The "standard" way to get preparation in today's culture is to go straight from high school to a four year university on borrowed money and take courses in something that you hope that you will like as you get older. If everyone is doing it, it probably won't pay off. You have to find ways of doing things that the herd is missing out on and go that way. I stumbled on another path and it worked out well for me.

I attended Arkansas State University for a while, but not enough to get a degree. I did get college English and instruction in writing. But I decided to get a trade first. I graduated Paramedical Medicine School at the Arkansas Community College. This took less time and money than a four year degree and gave me a technical trade to fall back on in case I hit some lean times in whatever profession I wound up in. I was a teacher/instructor for Eastman Kodak for a decade before I ran for Independence County Sheriff.

Eastman Kodak was an educational playground for me to learn and collect more education on the tab of corporate America. Yes, many companies still have programs where they help their employees get college courses. My point here is that instead of borrowing money and spending four years paying for college where you are earning nothing, try to get a trade and also get a job for a company which will work with you in obtaining your degree. Be open to the idea of obtaining higher education just like you obtain all other wealth- a little at a time without going into major debt to get there.

The university setting is not the only place to gain knowledge. Honestly, I graduated from a Dale Carnegie Course on public speaking and I would say that it was far more valuable in enhancing my communications skills than anything I learned in college. It set the stage for me to win election to the office of Sheriff and also my more lucrative careers in insurance and oil and gas pipeline negotiations.

Not that being a good talker is all that it takes. You have to go after your dream. When I ran for Sheriff I knocked on so many doors and walked around meeting people so regularly that I lost thirty pounds and wore out three pairs of shoes on the campaign! So being a good talker won't help you if you don't do the work of getting in front of the right people to talk to, but doing the work to get in front of them won't help if you don't know how to speak well when you get there!

The tuition for college in this day and time will put you in the poor house. Think twice about doing it with debt and consider something more like the path that I took. When I went to Emergency Medical Technician school it was a thrill and I enjoyed the adrenalin rush while making a living. After almost three years working as a medic in Helena Hospital in Helena, Arkansas I was offered a job in Batesville, Arkansas in 1986. I worked my way up to Assistant Director. Then I was offered a job at Eastman Kodak. Eastman was a wonderful ten year stint learning new technology. With my employer helping every step of the way, I attended Texas A & M University industrial fire science courses and also courses at LSU where I received a certification as an Industrial Fire Science instructor.

This was a great time of my life in the education field until I attended Dale Carnegie Course in Public Speaking. Public speaking seemed to be natural for me and I was looking at larger fish to fry- and by then I was prepared to fry those fish. If I had tried to run for Sheriff fresh out of college it would have been a bad joke. While Eastman had been very good to me and I obtained many college credits and educational classes it was time to move on. Eastman seemed to be experiencing difficulty and corporate American was down-sizing. Even in a place where you are happy, you have to be aware of when it is time to move on because nothing stays the same forever, especially not us!

The point I am making with this chapter is that I got into a corporation that funded my education and therefore, I did not have lingering debt to hold me back. I always took short courses and payed very little out of my pocket for education. Many corporations have programs to help you get an education because the kind of people they want working for them are those who are always looking to improve.

Colleges will drain your money and put your parents into the poor house if you let them. I had one friend that graduated with a bachelor's degree in forestry and could not even make $23,000 a year. Finally, he went on to be a police officer. He made maybe $40,000 a year when he retired. Basically, the college degree was wasted since it took five years to finish and about $30,000 a year to attend college. And he never even worked in his field! There are too many stories like that out there.

After I became the third youngest elected sheriff in Arkansas at age thirty-seven, I completed Arkansas Law Enforcement Training Academy and graduated from University of Arkansas Leadership School. I was a life-long learner, but the money for it was not coming out of my family's budget!

This career led me to Arkansas Insurance School and I obtained a multi-line license and series 6 and series 63 license for securities. I started my career in sales and was hired in 2003 in Farmers Ranch Health Insurance and attended a free school in Texas. This career served me until I was hired in 2005 as a Branch Manager in Springfield, Missouri with Bankers Life and Casualty.

I worked at this and earned a six-figure income until I was recruited to New York Life as a partner. This was at the top of my career. I was wearing a suit and tie to work each day and an office on the fifteenth floor overlooking the city. This was a career I dearly loved until 2008 hit and the game changed. Most everyone remembers this economic year as everything came to a screeching halt financially. A serious housing market crash occurred, so I had to look for a new avenue.

That is when I called a friend of mine named Rick. Rick told me what he was doing. He was negotiating pipeline agreements in the oil and gas business. All I had to do is offer people money within my guidelines and get the documents signed. I thought to myself, "I have been teaching agents for the last five years how to talk people out of their money, now I need to talk people into taking my money." This was a dream career and I made very good money doing it- allowing me to semi-retire at age 53. I never did get an actual four year college degree, but I did get an education.

I Ignore My Own Advice

It is confession time. I did not always follow my own advice. I got a little cocky and I had to learn a lesson. Hopefully you can benefit from my mistake and avoid getting in a similar situation. There are some people who can gamble with the banks and win- for a while. I am not one of them. To find out if you are, you have to risk falling into their hands.

In 2005, took a huge risk. I was completely debt free and decided to move my family to Missouri. I accepted a job as a manager for an insurance agency. My wife and children found a nice Victorian home about 15 minutes from the city of Springfield. I signed a lease for one year. During this process I was hoping to sell my home free and clear in Arkansas and buy the home we had leased. Everything seemed to be going great, so we decided to buy the home we were leasing even though we did not have the cash to pay for it. We *would have* the cash when our Arkansas home sold, but we had not sold it yet, and Batesville, Arkansas never was a hot area for real estate!

Ninety days after we closed on that home our twenty-two year marriage came to an abrupt end. I was going through a lot, and definitely did not need debt in my life! Still, I accepted both pieces of real estate in Arkansas and Missouri as my equity in the divorce.

I was doing everything possible to sell the Arkansas home but nothing seemed to work. Shortly after that, the bottom fell out of the real estate market in the 2008 crash. I said to myself a thousand times if I ever sell this Missouri home and get out of this trap I will never be in debt again, ever. I was so miserable being a slave and was praying every day to sell this house. It was not until 2010 that my prayers were answered and I sold the home outside of Springfield- I had to struggle with it long enough to make the lesson stick.

It was a wonderful day- one to be remembered. I was free at last from bondage. Waiting for my house to sell in Arkansas and pay off the house in Missouri was a refresher course in managing risk and debt. It was a hard lesson that I would not have had to re-learn if I had just stuck with the counsel of Mr. Huffine from all those years before. I wasted $36,000 on interest during those years. But look at the bright side, my credit score was so wonderful! That's just a little joke there. I could care less about my credit score, because I vowed to never sign myself into debt again, ever.

Mixed Reception from Pastors

In 1997, I attended a class taught by John Commuta in Chicago, Ill. John taught the principals of financial freedom and the importance of being debt free and staying out of debt. I earned two certifications from this school and was a certified financial planning specialist and financial seminar leader. It was one of the best educations in my life. Everything John taught me connected with what Mr. Huffine told me when I was seventeen.

After much preparation and study I was ready to teach. After graduation, I wanted to teach pastors and eventually reach out into their churches with my seminars. Some of my audiences were colleges, state emergency medical services personnel conventions, and a few churches.

Finally a group of Baptist Ministers ask me to teach the class so I saw this as my big opportunity to share my message. One pastor asked me to define debt and I said if you are in debt with credit cards, home mortgage or car payment you are in debt. The pastor had a different philosophy, he said if you have a two hundred thousand dollar home and you owe one hundred thousand you have one hundred thousand in the bank.

Well, he was kind of correct. You can only access that equity if the home sells (or if you go further in debt). Read the mortgage fine print, if the home sells for $150,000 you don't have $100,000, you have fifty thousand. And if it doesn't sell, every month it doesn't sell, you have a mortgage payment!

This pastor was named "Danny" and he was somewhat arrogant. He really gave me a hard time, not even the scriptures on debt impressed him. The pastors were Luke -warm at best in their response to my teaching. I got one invitation to speak from their group. But the real lesson I learned this day was invaluable. They asked me to define debt and I only gave them examples for an answer. I resolved to do better next time.

I was inspired to look up the word debt in the 9th edition of *Webster's College Dictionary* and this is what I saw: Debt; 1. Sin; trespass 2. to owe someone something for a good in return. Interesting enough, I looked at several dictionaries and this was the only dictionary definition I saw that debt was sin. But it fits with what it says in the Lord's Prayer, "forgive us our debts as we forgive our debtors" (King James Version). From that time forward, I answered the question "what is debt" more completely!

By the way, that was not the last I heard about "Pastor Danny", the one who challenged me to define debt. While I was sheriff, a pastor came to me and said "Pastor Danny was in charge of hundreds of thousands of dollars in church funds. Danny would receive a check from other churches for renting the Baptist Association Camp, dozens of people from other denominations would enjoy bunk houses and cafeteria and peace and serenity. However, when Pastor Danny received some of the checks to pay for it he would fail to deposit them into the Baptist Association checking account."

This was discovered when two pastors had just audited the books were in a local supermarket. The pastor from this other denomination came up and said, "thank you guys so much for the use of the camp last week. This camp fee was $6,000!" The two Baptist pastors did not remember seeing a check deposited last week that was received from Pastor Danny. They confronted him about it. Danny quickly asked for forgiveness and wanted to pay financial restitution, but Pastor Danny was estimated to have stolen hundreds of thousands of dollars over the course of his nine years as executive director. The group of thirty plus pastors voted not to prosecute Pastor Danny. Still, Pastor Danny was fired from his $85,000 a year plush job. I presume that he now knows very well what the definition of "debt" really is.

I started teaching class at Arkansas Community College and was somewhat dismayed that pastors did not buy into my teaching of debt freedom. I wanted to dig deeper and see why God's word was not important to the group I had spoken to earlier in my seminars. My pastor, Clyde Spurgin and I spoke to length and he shared with me deep financial secrets why America's pastors were not teaching the passages I mentioned earlier.

Clyde told me that a 501C3 ordained church and pastor received special tax treatment under federal law. He went on to say that for example if a lay person bought a duplex and a pastor bought a duplex and both were financed at the end of the fiscal year, let's say $5,000 was paid in interest on both parties, then the pastor had an advantage. The lay person can deduct $5,000 off his taxes but the ordained pastor can deduct $10,000 off of his taxes. Ordained ministers receive double indemnity for interest payments on debt. No wonder the USA has a $20 trillion dollar national debt and the people are in such bondage financially.

I guess if I was a pastor with this kind of federal tax benefit, I would be opposed to preaching Proverbs 22:7 as well. What an insidious way to undermine good financial sense in this nation because the conscience of the nation should echo from pulpits. I guess the banks got their money's worth out of that law because the people who should be warning folks the most about the dangers of debt are now too often silent. If you have a pastor who teachers you what the scripture says about debt then they should be doubly appreciated!

Frugal, Frugal, Frugal

"Madison Avenue" is the old-fashioned term for people in the marketing business. There are some very sharp people who work on Madison Avenue, both the literal one and figuratively. Brilliant and committed people wake up each and every day with one thing on their mind and that is to get your money. They will make what sounds like a compelling case as to why you simply must buy whatever it is they are selling, right now! Learn to take pleasure in frustrating them.

The late great Dorothy Sayers was off to a stellar career in marketing, until she lost her taste for it. She later said, "Of course, there is some truth in advertising. There's yeast in bread, but you can't make bread with yeast alone. Truth in advertising is like leaven, which a woman hid in three measures of meal. It provides a suitable quantity of gas, with which to blow out a mass of crude misrepresentation into a form that the public can swallow."

The key to avoid budgetary pit falls is learning to say "no". Sometimes you may have to ask a pushy sales person "what part of "no" don't you understand?" When purchasing any item if they try and sell me a warranty that I don't want (which is most of them), I have been known to tell them 'I may reconsider buying your product because you want to sell me a product you don't even believe in yourself'. Remember, there will always be another sale. You can say "no" today and if you really need it, you can get it later.

There is a special kind of joy and satisfaction in using the "envelope method" to train yourself how to save for consumption items you want. Let's say you want a new sofa. You need a new sofa. Rather than borrow the money to buy one that same day, you get an envelope and you write "Sofa" on it. Then every payday you take some cash, whatever you can save, and you put it in that envelope. And you keep doing that until one day, the money for that sofa is in your envelope! And then you go celebrate! You go out and buy that new sofa with joy because you have earned it! Celebrate those little financial victories. It helps get you motivated to win more of them. Stop and smell the roses along the way to wealth and prosperity.

Remember Mr. Huffine, the multi-millionaire, and the old coveralls he wore every day? This was a perfect example of a man with millions, but he was very frugal. He would wear a shirt ten years to get the value he spent. The Holy Bible says in Proverbs 13:7 – One person pretends to be rich and yet has nothing; another man appears to be poor and has great wealth. Kind of sounds like Mr. Huffine, doesn't it? But he had peace of mind. He did his children right. He had the freedom to help anyone he felt like he should help didn't he? What's worth more, all that or being a fashion plate everyday with credit card bills you can't pay?

Train yourself to take pleasure in preparing and eating meals at home instead of spending money in restaurants. Cooking, as long as you don't go too fancy, is a hobby that can save you money rather than cost you money. And believe me, a sure way to become poor is to develop a taste for expensive hobbies, and to spend lots of time pleasure-seeking. Actually, you don't have to take my word for it. Proverbs 21:17 says that those who love pleasure will become poor.

Being frugal doesn't always mean buying the cheapest. It means seeking the best value. Often that is not the cheapest item because the cheapest things don't have quality or durability. On the other hand, an item that is the most expensive in its class often has bells and whistles that don't add enough value to be worth the extra cost.

Now I want to add one more thing about cooking at home rather than eating out and it applies to what I said above too. Your body is your most important asset and you want to provide yourself with healthy, nutritious food. Sometimes that costs more than "junk" food. At the same time, an over-indulgence in delicacies can keep you poor whether purchased in a restaurant or grocery store.

Grocery stores have marketing people too, and some of them are getting pretty fancy. Food is a major expense and I advise making it a point to shop at stores that focus on selling you food at a reasonable price rather than a "beautiful experience" shopping for groceries! A potato is a potato. Why not get your groceries at Wal-Mart?

41

Now what I said above applies mostly to consumer goods. That us stuff you use up without making any money on it. It also applies to investment opportunities of two major kinds. One kind is a proposed investment by which they are telling you that you can "get rich quick." The other kind is an investment in a business you don't understand very well. Run from pitches in those two categories! Instead go to safer and surer investments in your youth.

The investment guys will tell you that the best time to invest in risky things is when you are young. I think it's the worst time because you have not learned how to evaluate risk very well when you are young. It may be when you are most gullible so that investment brokers can pitch you risky stuff, but it's not when you should buy risky stuff! When you are young what you have on your side is time. They will say you have time to recover from investment mistakes, but I say time is on your side to build wealth slowly and then when you get some seasoning and an area of expertise you are better prepared to spot when a risk is worth taking.

Once you develop your knowledge and skill in an area, spending money on investments quickly is good. When you invest wisely it is not really "spending", it is investing. In investing, you have the hope of getting a return from your spending, unlike normal consumer spending. There is nothing wrong about being decisive and investing when it is in an area you know something about.

Here is an example from my own life. I got real good at evaluating real estate. I could tell if a property was over-valued or under-valued. One day my ex-wife called and she said, "A lady in my office said she has a house for sale by the local college". Even though our marriage was over, we were still on good terms and wished the best for each other, so when she heard of an opportunity that I might be interested in she let me know about it.

I asked her for the address, and she told me. So I drove over to the house. I looked inside and said, "This is a bargain." I almost had a wreck trying to get to a pay phone to call her before the owner left my ex's office. I told her I would take the house. I kept this house two years and rented it out. Thirty months later I sold it, earning $12,000 profit. When you learn what the right moves to make are, you can move fast on investment "spending".

The point I am trying to make is this- look for deals but know when to say "no" and never go back once you make your mind up. These salesmen are sharp and convincing and they have one objective and that is to get your money into their pocket. As a rule of thumb, if you are not sure – walk away and don't look back.

The Most Important Decision this Side of Heaven- Marriage

This book is primarily about finances, but it would not be complete without talking about the most important decision most people ever make- marriage. I'd say that marrying the right person is about half the value of your adult life. If you do that one right you can still have a good life even if the rest of it goes wrong. If you get that one wrong, it is hard to have a good life even if you do the rest of it right. Instead of asking the richest man in town about money when I was your age, maybe I should have found the most successful couple in town and asked them about marriage! I have learned a lot about it over the years- some of it the hard way.

I was a young twenty-two year old man. I met a lady when I was twenty-one and dated for seven short months and we got married on January 1, 1985. She was twenty and still living at home. I was successful for my age. I had a paid for sports car (a Trans-Am), about $6,000 in the bank and was completely debt free. I worked at a local hospital in Helena, Arkansas as a paramedic. Life was good.

Dan Johnson

During our engagement, I was checking out all the important stuff. She was a Methodist. I attended and worshiped at the Baptist Church, so I felt they were compatible. Her parents were respectable as they were both professors at a local college. I really enjoyed talking with her dad and played tennis with her mother. We both wanted a boy and girl after marriage and everything was looking very good.

We talked about our expectations for debt and who would make what decisions. In retrospect, I probably should have checked her out for compatibility before we got so close. I mean we had over twenty good years together before things went south, but we were both very young and it is hard to know who you really are at that age. This can mask problems in compatibility which will only come out as each person figures out who they are. I didn't appreciate that as much as I should have at the time. The lesson is that you can think you are doing due diligence even if you aren't. We can save ourselves a lot of trouble if we quit kidding our self.

We rented our first home at $165 a month. After five years I got an offer to work as a paramedic at Eastman Kodak. This was an extreme blessing as my income rose about $25,000 per year. Shortly after I went to work with Eastman we discovered we were expecting our first child. So it was time to find our own home. I set out to look but nothing was affordable and appealing at the same time. Our daughter was born on December 19, 1988 and we had accumulated about $15,000 cash and we were still renting with zero debt.

Finally, we found our dream home- because we kept our dreams realistic and in budget. It was built in 1832 and needed to be completely remodeled. This was our home for the next fifteen years. We paid it off in five years and eleven months after purchase and remodeling. We never had any credit card bills so we did not have to stress out over debt.

I revert back to debt with marriage because studies show that in 57% of divorces finances and the stress of debt is a factor. The couples have a brief satisfaction when buying a new car, house or vacation but paying for it later brings on stress, and then divorce comes because of the blame game.

There was a Church of Christ preacher back in Arkansas who said "There are two kinds of women in this world, women who get a kick out of spending money and women who get a kick out of saving it. Do yourself a favor and marry one who gets a kick out of saving it." Reverse the sexes and the advice is the same. Big spenders may seem like fun people while courting, but responsible people are the most fun to have an actual life partnership with. It wears on one's nerves to have to be the "parent" to your spouse.

Ultimately, in spite of everything I thought that I did right, our marriage did not last. What I needed as a young man was someone who was to marriage advice like Mr. Huffine was to financial advice. I did not meet that person when I was young, but I have met him since. I have a dear friend that waited until he was about forty to marry. He met the love of his life and they now have three beautiful children.

Dan Johnson

He said they dated a year before even kissing- at their wedding ceremony. You know they married for the right reasons, and it shows.

I don't advise you wait as long as he did to get married, and he may not either, but it is ok if you do. Heck its ok if you stay single, so long as you can behave yourself. Don't go into marriage looking to change the other person, or yourself. There is a lot about people that marriage itself does not change! Don't count on your partner to fix whatever is wrong with you, and don't count on you being able to fix whatever is wrong with them. That's the Holy Spirit's job, and you are not as qualified for it as He!

My friend's advice on searching for a partner can be summed up as follows: "Seek character first, compatibility second, and then as much of everything else as you can get."

Now his wife is an attractive woman, and very sharp. So apparently he was able to get quite a bit of "everything else", but what he says is that he did not even let himself get sucked into a deep relationship until *after* he had established that someone he might be interested in had good character. Then he could evaluate their compatibility honestly. Even if they seemed compatible, without good character it would not mean much. Maybe they are just trying to appear compatible until the deal is sealed. Without character, you can't be sure of anything else.

Now he did not even do a lot of dating in his late twenties and thirties because good character was hard to find. When he did date he didn't do it long if he found the compatibility was not there. There was no point in carrying on with a person that you knew you would have to distance yourself from later. And of course by the time he met her, he knew who he was and so it was easier to tell if they were compatible on what mattered.

They did not kiss until their wedding day, so obviously they were not being led on by their hormones- that was icing on the cake for people who wanted to be together even without the physical aspect of the relationship. He said if a woman tried to lead with what should follow, it was a huge red flag. If a woman hated her father, it was a huge red flag. If they loved pleasure or experiences more than God or people, it was a red flag. Such people are fun to be around for a season, but for a partner you want someone who cares about people more than pleasure. This is a man who walks in the light of the Word of God and his advice on marriage reflects the ultimate source of his wisdom.

Let me add that "compatibility" doesn't always mean being alike. Sometimes even the differences can be good. Say one was weak in an area where the other was strong. Sometimes those are differences which balance you out and make the couple greater than the sum of the parts. Sometimes those differences come to be an obstacle. Evaluate your differences and figure out which are which! And despite that, the very best situation is that both partners are balance people and merely enhance each other overall. Try to be the kind of person you want to be married to and you will attract that kind!

Final Remarks

A picture from soon after I was sworn in as Sheriff: I had my big moments and you can have yours too!

The primary objective of this book is to teach you the importance of staying and remaining debt-free. I cannot emphasize enough the time you will capture in peace of mind throughout your life. Always remember knowledge is power, power is money, and money is freedom, so long as it is enjoyed without sin. A credit score is nothing more than a tool interjected into society so that the slave owners can determine how good a slave you are when they are trying to get you on the hook to them.

Our money says "in God We Trust". I don't think the people behind that money really believe it anymore, but it's what I believe. I am willing to have patience to get nice things rather than go into debt to another man in order to have them now. I figure when the time is right, when I can have them and they won't ruin me, the Good Lord will give me the money to pay for them. I should not have to sell myself into the service of another for them. My wish for you is to know the freedom and peace I have enjoyed in life, and be spared the pain of avoidable mistakes.

Finally, let's not forget that money is not an end in itself. Life is not about just piling up as much stuff as we can before we pass on. Jesus said "Give and it shall be given unto you." The measure we give is the measure we get in return.

Gaining wealth allows us to help people, which is another kind of wealth in itself. When you see someone hungry, you can feed them. If they have no shelter, you can shelter them. If they are without clothes, you can give them your old clothes. All my years I have seen people who do these things be taken care of throughout life. I have seen others who helped only themselves and yet they still came to ruin. It doesn't make sense at first that the generous person winds up being taken care of while the one who keeps all their treasures here runs out, but I've seen it.

Not that giving to the poor will always give you "warm fuzzies". A woman named Dorothy Day was famous for her work helping poor people. When an idealistic young couple came to her with a desire to help her in her work she said, "There are two things you ought to know about the poor, they tend to smell, and they are ungrateful." It is about doing the right thing for the right reasons. It is about you becoming a grateful and giving person, not being gushed over.

You can never tell how someone you are trying to help will react. When I was in my early twenties I was sitting on my front porch in Desha, Arkansas. I rented a house there for $200 a month. It is flat country, Delta Country, and there was nothing but a long stretch of highway on both sides of my home. I looked to my right and a man was walking by. He looked very dirty and hungry, and was shoeless.

I said "wait a moment and I will get you some shoes." I stepped in my house, looked in the closet and grabbed an old pair of shoes. I walked back out and he had vanished. I was not gone but maybe half a minute. There was no place to hide and no way that he could have walked out of sight so fast. He vanished into thin air. I was reminded of the scripture in Hebrews (13:2) which says that some have "entertained angels unaware."

Maybe it was an angel and maybe just a dirty hobo who was so good at getting away that not even the future Sheriff of Independence County, Arkansas could spot him!

53

Dan Johnson

Either way, I was financially blessed in whatever I set my hand to from that day forward. And I wanted to share more than shoes, I wanted to share, with you, the best counsel I have heard that helped me get there.

Yours in Him,

Dan Johnson

If you want Dan to speak at your event email him here... sheriffdanjohnson@gmail.com ....

Notes

What is the number one lesson you learned from this book?

What is something you are going to do differently after reading this book?

What is the advantage of building wealth slowly over using high risk tactics to get it quickly?

What are some of your financial goals?